Boo

MW00782869

IN RECITAL®
with Classical Themes
Volume One

ABOUT THE SERIES • A NOTE TO THE TEACHER

In Recital® with Classical Themes is devoted to timeless classical music. The fine arrangers of this series were commissioned to create engaging solo and duet arrangements of classical themes, according to strict pedagogical guidelines. The result is a series that is artistically strong, carefully leveled, and pedagogically sound. We know that to motivate, the teacher must challenge the student with attainable goals. This series makes that possible while also providing a perfect way for students to discover and enjoy classical music themes. You will find favorite themes from symphonies, operas, chamber music, choral music, as well as from advanced piano concertos and piano duets. This series complements other FJH publications and can be used alongside any method. Students will find even more joy in these classical themes when they read about the pieces (a brief history is provided at the beginning and end of each book).

Use the downloadable recordings as a teaching and motivational tool. Have your students listen to the recording and discuss interpretation with you! Also encourage your students to listen to the works in their original format. Turn to the inside back cover for instructions on downloading the tracks related to this book.

THE
F·J·H
MUSIC
COMPANY
I N C.

Frank J. Hackinson

Production: Frank J. Hackinson
Production Coordinators: Joyce Loke and Philip Groeber
Art Direction: Terpstra Design, San Francisco, in collaboration with Helen Marlais
Cover and Inside Illustrations: Keith Criss
Engraving: Tempo Music Press, Inc.
Printer: Tempo Music Press, Inc.

ISBN-13: 978-1-56939-652-0

ORGANIZATION OF THE SERIES
IN RECITAL® WITH CLASSICAL THEMES

The series is carefully leveled into the following six categories: Early Elementary, Elementary, Late Elementary, Early Intermediate, Intermediate, and Late Intermediate. Each of the works has been selected for its artistic as well as its pedagogical merit.

Book Three — Late Elementary, reinforces the following concepts:

■ Introduction of eighth notes and eighth note rests.

■ Students reinforce their comprehension of tonic and dominant notes and basic chord progressions.

■ Five-finger patterns as well as patterns that extend from a five-finger pattern are used.

■ Reinforcement of blocked and broken chords and intervals.

■ Musical details (*crescendi* and *ritardandos*).

■ Keys — C major, G major, D major, F major, A minor, and D minor (using key signatures).

Most of the classical themes in this book were arranged as solos. Some of them include teacher accompaniments. There are three equal-part duets— *The Little Man in the Woods, Marche Slav,* and *The Dance of the Hours.*

FJH1699

TABLE OF CONTENTS

About the Pieces and Composers

"London" Symphony, by Franz Joseph Haydn (1732-1809)

Franz Joseph Haydn wrote over 100 symphonies, and this particular symphony was his last. He composed this piece while living in London, England in 1795. The premiere (first performance) was a great success, making Haydn very popular in London. Haydn was nicknamed "Papa Haydn" because all the musicians with whom he worked liked him so much. After 1761 he worked as court composer for a royal family named Esterházy throughout his lifetime. His mastery of the symphony earned him the title "father of the symphony."

String Quartet, by Franz Joseph Haydn (1732-1809)

The melody of this theme is famous because it is the tune of the Austrian national anthem, known as *The Emperor's Hymn*, which Haydn composed in 1797. A string quartet is made up of two violinists, a violist, and a cellist. If you played in a string quartet, which instrument would you like to play? Not only is Haydn considered to be the "father of the symphony," but he is also considered to be the "father of the string quartet!"

Ode to Joy, by Ludwig van Beethoven (1770-1827)

Beethoven is considered one of the most important composers of all time. He was born in Bonn, Germany, studied with Haydn for a time, and settled in Vienna, Austria, which was the center for music at the time. The famous *Ode to Joy* theme is from Beethoven's *Ninth Symphony*. As a young boy, Beethoven was inspired by a poem by Schiller about faith and hope. Later in life, he decided to set the poem to music and this became the *Ode to Joy*. In the symphony, four soloists and a chorus sing the words while a full orchestra accompanies. The piece was dedicated to the King of Prussia, Friedrich Wilhelm III, and the original score bears his coat of arms. Beethoven composed this work after he became deaf, which is a terrible thing for anyone, but especially difficult for a musician.

The Royal March of the Lion, by Camille Saint-Saëns (1835-1921)

The Royal March of the Lion is a lively piece that is part of a fourteen-movement work entitled *Carnival of the Animals*. It was written for two pianists and a small orchestra. Each movement depicts different animals—such as tortoises, elephants, kangaroos, birds, and swans. In this particular arrangement, do you hear the lion roar when you listen to the recording? Camille Saint-Saëns was a French composer, conductor, pianist, and organist. His mother and an aunt taught him to play the piano when he was just three years old. He began to compose at the early age of five, and his first public performance at the age of ten included concertos by Beethoven and Mozart.

FJH1699

The Little Man in the Woods, by Engelbert Humperdinck (1854-1921)

This sweet little piece is from the opera *Hansel and Gretel.* In the spring of 1890, a writer named Adelheid Wette wanted to produce a children's play for her family. She asked her brother, the composer Engelbert Humperdink, if he might write a tune to some lines of verse. She was so pleased with the piece that she conceived the idea of a little family opera based on Grimm's fairy tale *Hansel and Gretel.* As Wette and Humperdink worked on it, the piece grew into a full-sized opera, which they completed in 1893.

Hansel and Gretel is an enchanting story of two children sent into the woods by their mother to search for strawberries in a time of scarcity. They are able to find their way home by leaving a trail of pebbles. The next time they are sent out, they leave a trail of breadcrumbs, which is eaten by the birds. Wandering around lost in the woods, they came upon a beautiful house built of cakes and sugar. Little did they know, it was the home of a wicked witch, who captures the children and plans to eat them when they are fattened up. Gretel is able to trick the witch, and they are both able to escape.

Now I Lay Me Down To Sleep, by Engelbert Humperdinck (1854-1921)

In this piece, *Hansel and Gretel* fall asleep after being lost in the woods. Fourteen angels watch over them to protect them through the night. The composer Engelbert Humperdinck was born in Germany, and studied in two beautiful cities, Cologne and Munich.

"LONDON" SYMPHONY
(Symphony in D major, Hob. 104, Movement One)

Franz Joseph Haydn
arr. Kevin Olson

* This is an *espressivo* marking, which means to play the note with tenderness, emotion, and extra warmth.

FJH1699

STRING QUARTET
(Kaiser, Opus 76, No. 3, Movement Two)

Franz Joseph Haydn
arr. Robert Schultz

Poco adagio cantabile (♩ = ca. 84)

FJH1699

ODE TO JOY

from *Symphony No. 9, Opus 125, Movement Four*

Ludwig van Beethoven
arr. Timothy Brown

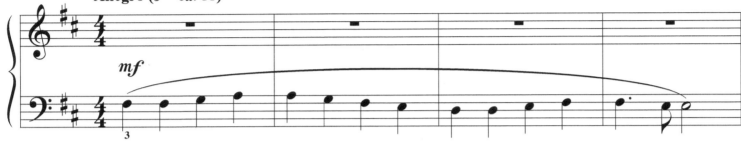

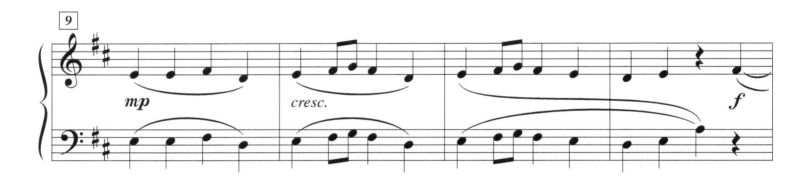

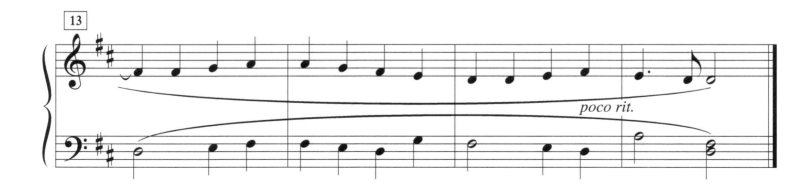

FJH1699

THE ROYAL MARCH OF THE LION
from *Carnival of the Animals*

Camille Saint-Saëns
arr. Edwin McLean

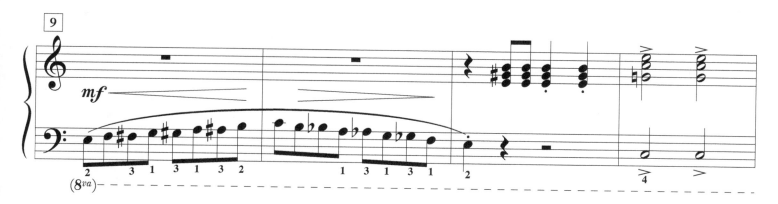

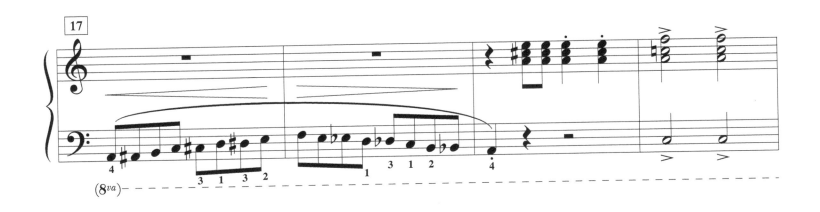

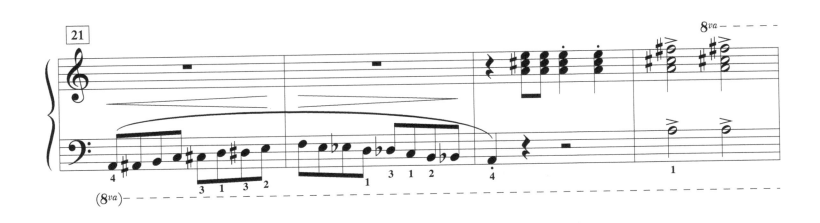

FJH1699

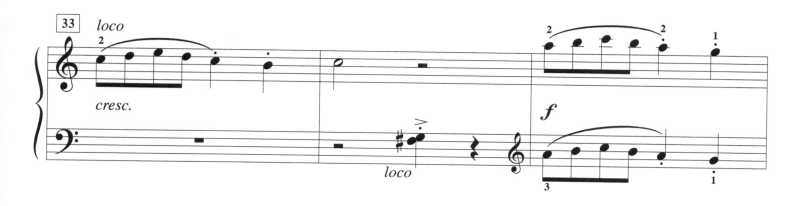

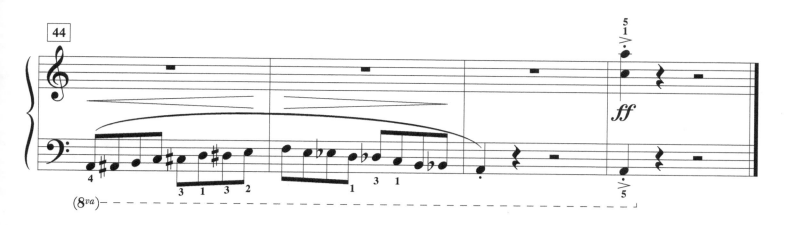

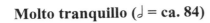

THE LITTLE MAN IN THE WOODS

from *Hansel and Gretel*

Secondo

Engelbert Humperdinck
arr. Kevin Olson

Molto tranquillo (♩ = ca. 84)

Play both hands 1 octave lower throughout

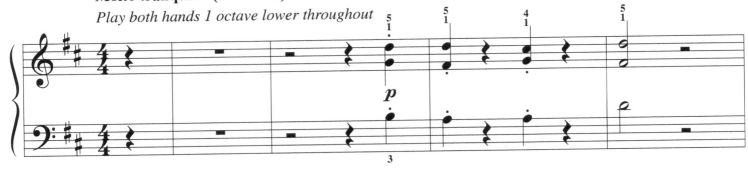

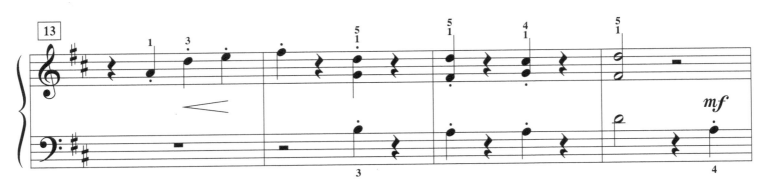

FJH1699

THE LITTLE MAN IN THE WOODS

from *Hansel and Gretel*

Primo

Engelbert Humperdinck
arr. Kevin Olson

Molto tranquillo (♩ = ca. 84)

Play both hands 1 octave higher throughout

FJH1699

Secondo

FJH1699

Primo

Now I Lay Me Down To Sleep

from *Hansel and Gretel*

Secondo

Teacher Part

Engelbert Humperdinck
arr. Robert Schultz

FJH1699

NOW I LAY ME DOWN TO SLEEP

from *Hansel and Gretel*

Primo

Student Part

Engelbert Humperdinck
arr. Robert Schultz

FJH1699

17

Secondo

Primo

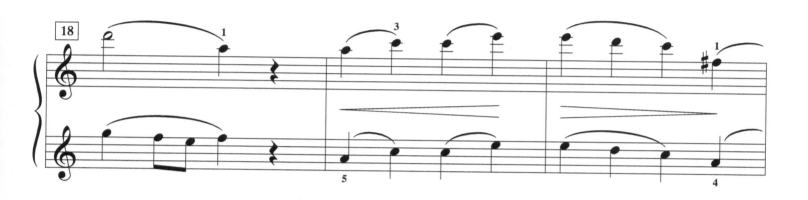

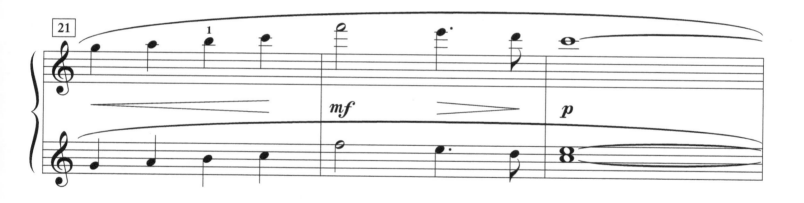

EINE KLEINE NACHTMUSIK
(*A Little Night Music, K. 525, Movement Three*)

Wolfgang Amadeus Mozart
arr. David Karp

Allegretto (♩ = ca. 120)

Teacher Accompaniment: (*Student plays one octave higher*)

FJH1699

SHEEP MAY SAFELY GRAZE

from *Birthday Cantata, BWV 208, Movement Nine*

Secondo
Student Part

Johann Sebastian Bach
arr. Edwin McLean

FJH1699

SHEEP MAY SAFELY GRAZE

from *Birthday Cantata, BWV 208, Movement Nine*

Primo
Teacher Part

Johann Sebastian Bach
arr. Edwin McLean

*Start the trill on the upper note.

FJH1699

Secondo

24

Primo

POLOVTSIAN DANCE NO. 17

from *Prince Igor*

Alexander Borodin
arr. Mary Leaf

Teacher Accompaniment: (*Student plays one octave higher*)

FJH1699

THE DANCE OF THE HOURS

from *La Gioconda*

Secondo

Amilcare Ponchielli
arr. Robert Schultz

FJH1699

THE DANCE OF THE HOURS

from *La Gioconda*

Primo

Amilcare Ponchielli
arr. Robert Schultz

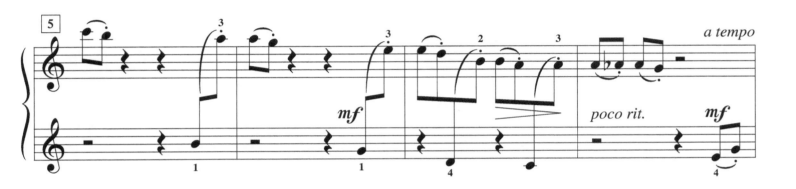

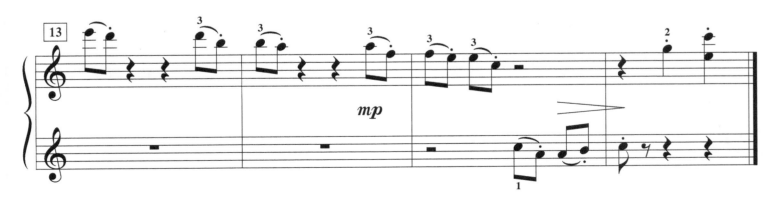

FJH1699

29

MARCHE SLAV
(Opus 31)

Secondo

Pyotr Ilyich Tchaikovsky
arr. Timothy Brown

FJH1699

MARCHE SLAV
(Opus 31)

Primo

Pyotr Ilyich Tchaikovsky
arr. Timothy Brown

Moderato (♩ = ca. 112)

Play both hands 1 octave higher throughout

VIOLIN CONCERTO
(Opus 77, Movement Two)

Johannes Brahms
arr. Kevin Olson

FJH1699

ABOUT THE PIECES AND COMPOSERS

Eine kleine Nachtmusik, by Wolfgang Amadeus Mozart (1756-1791)

Mozart composed *A Little Night Music* for string quartet: two violins, a viola, a cello, and a bass. *A Little Night Music* originally had five movements, or sections, but now only four exist because the second movement was lost. After each movement, the performers rest briefly before they begin the next movement. If you were watching and listening to musicians play this piece, you would only clap at the very end of the piece, not after each movement. Mozart wrote this famous piece while living in Vienna and it was completed on August 10, 1787. During this time he was also writing one of his most famous operas, *Don Giovanni*. A piano arrangement of the third movement of *A Little Night Music* is found in this book. It is a minuet, so it needs to sound graceful, short and simple, with a flowing melody.

Sheep May Safely Graze, by Johann Sebastian Bach (1685-1750)

Johann Sebastian Bach composed *Sheep May Safely Graze* in 1713. It is part of a larger work for chorus and orchestra, called *The Hunting Cantata* or *Birthday Cantata*. It was written in celebration of a Duke's birthday (Duke Christian of Sachsen-Weissenfels) in Germany. Bach was born in Eisenach, Germany to a large and distinguished family of musicians who were prominent for over 300 years! Bach was a superb organist and harpsichordist, and a genius as a composer, whose compositions number over a thousand.

Polovtsian Dance No. 17, by Alexander Borodin (1833-1887)

One of Borodin's greatest achievements was his opera *Prince Igor*. This arrangement of the *Polovtsian Dance* is found in this opera. Listen to the CD recording to understand the spirit and excitement of the work. The Russian composer Borodin was a chemist by profession. He learned the flute, cello, and piano, and began to experiment with composing in his teens. When his mother married a physician, he became interested in chemistry, and he spent his life in two spheres: he had a distinguished career in science as a professor at the St. Petersburg Medical-Surgical Academy, and he had an encompassing hobby in music. Borodin's music is highly colorful.

FJH1699

The Dance of the Hours, by Amilcare Ponchielli (1834-1886)

The Dance of the Hours is a famous theme. The work is from a ballet called *La Gioconda*, composed by an Italian named Ponchielli. He studied at the Milan Conservatory in Italy and became a professor of composition there. Ponchielli was a leading composer of opera. An opera is a dramatic work that combines music, poetry, action, drama, visual art, and stagecraft. In 1876, *La Gioconda* was first performed in Milan, Italy, at the famous and beautiful La Scala opera house.

Marche Slav, by Pyotr Ilyich Tchaikovsky (1840-1893)

This piece in its original form is played by four flutes, two oboes, two clarinets, two bassoons, four horns, four trumpets, three trombones, tuba, timpani, four percussion instruments, and strings. The Russian Czar asked Tchaikovsky to compose an orchestral piece for a benefit concert honoring wounded soldiers from Serbia after Turkey invaded their country. This piece, composed in 1876, is a patriotic march and should be played with pride, enthusiasm, and zeal.

Violin Concerto, by Johannes Brahms (1833-1897)

Brahms' *Concerto for Violin and Orchestra* was composed in 1878 at a lakeside village that Brahms used as his summer residence. A violin concerto is a piece for a solo violinist and orchestra. The first movement is fast, the second is slow, and the third is fast again. The theme in this book is from the second (slow) movement. Brahms' *Violin Concerto* is serene, and demands great skill on the part of the violinist. Maybe one day soon you will go to a concert where a violin concerto is being performed! Despite a modest upbringing, Brahms' parents sent him to private elementary and secondary schools, where he had a superior education and developed a lifelong love of learning. Johannes Brahms is one of the great composers of the Romantic era.

Timothy Brown

Timothy Brown holds a master's degree in piano performance from the University of North Texas, where he studied piano with Adam Wodnicki and music composition with Newel Kay Brown. He was later a recipient of a research fellowship from the Royal Holloway, University of London, where he performed postgraduate studies in music composition and orchestration, studying with English composer Brian Lock. His numerous credits as a composer include first prize at the Aliénor International Harpsichord Competition for his harpsichord solo *Suite Española* (Centaur Records). Mr. Brown leads a very active career as an exclusive composer and clinician for The FJH Music Company Inc.

Mr. Brown's works have been performed by concert artist Elaine Funaro on NPR, and most recently at the Spoleto Music Festival and the Library of Congress Concert Series in Washington, D.C. His numerous commissions include a commission by *Clavier* Magazine for his piano solo *Once Upon a Time*, edited by Denes Agay. Mr. Brown is currently a fine arts specialist for the Dallas Public Schools and serves on the advisory board of the Booker T. Washington High School for the Performing and Visual Arts in Dallas, Texas.

David Karp

David Karp, nationally known pianist, composer, educator, lecturer, and author, holds degrees from the Manhattan School of Music and the University of Colorado. Dr. Karp is professor of music and director of the National Piano Teachers Institute at the Meadows School of the Arts where he teaches courses in piano performance, composition, theory and aural skills, improvisation, and class piano techniques for the college teacher. He has performed, lectured, and conducted workshops and seminars at many colleges and universities from Alaska to New Hampshire and as far away as Taiwan.

In 1993, Dr. Karp was honored with the establishment of the David Karp Piano Festival, an annual event held at Kilgore College in Kilgore, Texas, in which over 200 students perform and are judged on Karp compositions. He has also been a guest artist and clinician as well as commissioned composer for the South Dakota and North Dakota MTA state conventions. Dr. Karp recently performed and recorded Simon Sargon's *Divertimento for Piano and Chamber Orchestra* (Gasparo Records), which was released Spring 2003.

Mary Leaf

Mary Leaf is an independent piano teacher specializing in early elementary through intermediate level students. She enjoys writing music that is descriptive, expressive, imaginative, and fun, while still being musically sound.

Mary received a music education degree from the University of Washington and has done continuing education in pedagogy at North Dakota State University. She has composed and arranged music for a family recorder ensemble, and has been active as a performer, accompanist, handbell ringer, and choir member at her church. She is also active in area contests as an accompanist. Mary and her husband Ron have five children and live in Bismarck, North Dakota.

Edwin McLean

Edwin McLean is a composer living in Chapel Hill, North Carolina. He is a graduate of the Yale School of Music, where he studied with Krzysztof Penderecki and Jacob Druckman. He also holds a master's degree in music theory and a bachelor's degree in piano performance from the University of Colorado.

Mr. McLean has authored over 200 publications for The FJH Music Company, ranging from *The FJH Classic Music Dictionary* to original works for pianists from beginner to advanced. His highly-acclaimed works for harpsichord have been performed internationally and are available on the Miami Bach Society recording, *Edwin McLean: Sonatas for 1, 2, and 3 Harpsichords*. His 2011 solo jazz piano album *Don't Say Goodbye* (CD1043) includes many of his advanced works for piano published by FJH.

Edwin McLean began his career as a professional arranger. Currently, he is senior editor for The FJH Music Company Inc.

Kevin Olson

Kevin Olson is an active pianist, composer, and member of the piano faculty at Utah State University, where he has taught a variety of courses, including piano literature, pedagogy, and accompanying. In addition to his collegiate teaching responsibilities, Kevin is a faculty advisor for the Utah State University Youth Conservatory, which provides weekly group and private piano instruction to more than 200 pre-college community students. The National Association of Schools of Music has recently recognized the Conservatory as a model for pre-college piano instruction programs. Before teaching at Utah State, he was on the faculty at Elmhurst College near Chicago and Humboldt State University in northern California.

A native of Utah, Kevin began composing at age five. When he was twelve, his composition, *An American Trainride,* received the Overall First Prize at the 1983 National PTA Convention at Albuquerque, New Mexico. Since then he has been a Composer in Residence at the National Conference on Keyboard Pedagogy, and has written music commissioned and performed by groups such as the American Piano Quartet, the American Festival Chorus and Orchestra, Chicago a cappella, the Rich Matteson Jazz Festival, Music Teachers National Association, and several piano teacher associations around the country.

Kevin maintains a large piano studio, teaching students of a variety of ages and abilities. Many of the needs of his own piano students have inspired more than 100 books and solos published by the FJH Music Company, which he joined as a writer in 1994.

Robert Schultz

Robert Schultz, composer, arranger, and editor, has achieved international fame during his career in the music publishing industry. The Schultz Piano Library, established in 1980, has included more than 500 publications of classical works, popular arrangements, and Schultz's original compositions in editions for pianists of every level from the beginner through the concert artist. In addition to his extensive library of published piano works, Schultz's output includes original orchestral works, chamber music, works for solo instruments, and vocal music.

Schultz has presented his published editions at workshops, clinics, and convention showcases throughout the United States and Canada. He is a long-standing member of ASCAP and has served as president of the Miami Music Teachers Association. Mr. Schultz's original piano compositions and transcriptions are featured on the compact disc recordings *Visions of Dunbar* and *Tina Faigen Plays Piano Transcriptions,* released on the ACA Digital label and available worldwide. His published original works for concert artists are noted in Maurice Hinson's *Guide to the Pianist's Repertoire, Third Edition.* He currently devotes his full time to composing and arranging, writing from his studio in Miami, Florida.

FJH1699

FUN WITH CLASSICAL THEMES

With your teacher, choose two or three of the classical themes from this book to play for an audience.

Write your pieces here:

Title of piece: Composer's Name:

_____

_____

_____

Your biography (25 words or less)

_____

_____

_____

Where are you going to play? (Circle any of these)

For family	For friends	For piano teacher
For piano group class	At church	At school
At a nursing home	For a pet	Other: _____

Now you can prepare for another classical theme playing event!